FOLLOW-UP QUESTIONS & COMMENTS FOR KIDS WITH AUTISM & ASPERGER'S

SIX-MINUTE CONVERSATION SKILLS

WORKBOOK

Print ISBN 978-1-989505-08-3

Ebook ISBN 978-1-989505-09-0

Happy Frog Press

www.HappyFrogPress.com

TABLE OF CONTENTS

INTRODUCTION

In this workbook, your learner will practice three types of conversational responses.

- Short Comments
- Follow-up Comments
- Follow-up Questions

Short comments are brief comments like "Interesting" or "Cool." Their main purpose is to show that we are listening and attending to the speaker.

A follow-up comment is a comment where the listener adds information relevant to what was just said.

A follow-up question is a question that is related to the current topic of conversation.

Your learner will practice these individually, and then combine them gradually to make real, multi-turn conversations that are on-topic and relevant.

WHY LEARN THESE SKILLS

These three response types are the key to maintaining a conversation topic.

The ability to maintain a conversation is vital for all learners. Conversations are how we get to know people, develop and maintain relationships, and build connections to reach our short and long term goals at any age.

Support your struggling speakers with this fun, engaging workbook that will build your learner's ability and confidence in this important skill.

ABOUT THIS WORKBOOK

Key details of this workbook are:

- Suitable for 1-1 or group use

  This book can be used in a group or with a single learner.

- Gradually increments difficulty

  Learners begin with simple commenting and questioning tasks, which gradually increment in difficulty as the book progresses. By the end, learners will be able to maintain a conversation topic for multiple turns.

- No-prep. No extra materials required

Everything needed is included in the book. You can get
started right now.

- Small chunks. Use any time

Our worksheets are designed for 'six-minute sessions.'
Anytime you have a spare moment, your learner can
accomplish the next incremental step in their learning
journey.

NEED MORE HELP?

If your learner needs more support with conversation and
friendship, consider the following workbooks, also from Happy
Frog Press.

The Conversation Skills workbook covers similar content to this
workbook but introduces additional skills as well as introducing
the skills more gradually.

HOW TO COACH A SIX-MINUTE SESSION

No student wants to spend extra time learning. Follow the guidelines in this section to promote efficient and motivating progress for your student.

1. Have a consistent and regular schedule

Consistency and regularity are vital if you want to reach a goal. So, choose a regular schedule for your six-minute sessions, get your learner's agreement and stick to it!

In a school setting, make this task a regular part of your students' day. In a home setting, aim for 3-4 times per week.

2. Devise a reward system

Working on skill deficits is hard work for any learner. Appreciate your student's effort by building in a reward system.

This may include a reward when a specific number of exercises are finished, when tasks are completed correctly on the first try, or whatever specific goal will encourage your learner at this point in their journey.

Remember to reward based on effort as well as correctness.

3. Scaffold then fade for success

As your learner encounters a new challenge, scaffold the task so your learner can be successful.

For example, if your student can't think of a follow-up question, try giving alternatives, "Why don't you ask a WHEN or a WHERE question?"

Later in the same session, try the same example and/or a similar example without scaffolding.

Your learner is ready to move on to the next section when they can achieve 80% success without scaffolding.

4. Don't write in the book

What? It's a workbook, isn't it?

Well, yes. But your student will learn more if you complete this workbook orally. Instead of writing the answer, require your learner to answer as if in a real conversation.

Your learner's brain will work hard, but he or she will develop skills that are immediately generalizable.

In fact, the best use of the workbook is for you to use it for notes.

- Identify any tasks that were challenging and make sure to add a few similar task later.
- Cross out and replace words/situations that are not relevant or appropriate for your learner.

- Make note of additional situations/examples that are particularly relevant to your learner.

5. Most importantly....

Most importantly, make this a FUN experience with your learner!

Learning happens best when our brains are relaxed - not stressed. It is your job to make sure your student's brain stays ready to learn while doing this workbook. Build success upon success and celebrate every small achievement.

MAKE A SHORT
COMMENT

Short comments are brief comments like "Interesting" or "Cool". Their main purpose is to show that we are listening and attending to the speaker.

Instead of words, listeners can also nod or glance at the speaker to show that they are listening.

If we don't show we are listening, it looks like we are bored or not listening. The speaker might feel hurt or angry because he thinks we are ignoring him.

In this section, your student practices making short comments and actions that show he/she is listening and empathize with the speaker.

We recommend you go over the following key points with your learner.

WHAT:

- **Short comments** are brief comments like "Interesting" or "Cool" or "That's too bad."

WHY:

- Short comments show you are listening and interested.
- Speakers feel good when they know you are interested.

HOW:

- Use a variety of responses, not just the same one over and over.
- Your comment should match the emotion of your friend's conversation.
- You don't always have to say something, you can use your eyes and your body to show you are listening.

Add a short comment to show you are listening.

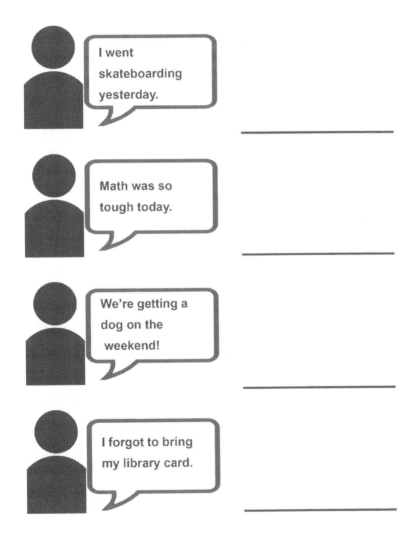

Add a short comment to show you are listening.

Add a short comment to show you are listening.

Add a short comment to show you are listening.

Add a short comment to show you are listening.

SHORT COMMENTS: REVIEW

I used my body or my words to show I was listening.

I varied my responses.

I matched the speaker's emotion.

MAKE A FOLLOW-UP COMMENT

A follow-up comment is a comment where the speaker adds some information relevant to what was just said.

For example:

A: I went clothes shopping on the weekend.

B: Hey, so did I!

In this conversation the 'so did I' is a follow-up comment. It is relevant additional information to the topic that speaker A introduced.

Follow-up comments can be used instead of, or in addition to, short comments.

In this section, students practice making follow-up comments.

We recommend you go over the following key points with your learner.

WHAT:

- A **follow-up comment** is when you add additional information related to what your friend just said.

WHY:

- Follow-up comments keep the conversation going.
- Follow-up questions show you are listening and interested.
- Speakers feel good when they know you are interested.

HOW:

- Your comment must be **related** to what your friend just said.
- Your question should be related to **your friend's topic**, not your own special interest.
- Occasionally, **look at your friend briefly** when you begin the comment so he knows you are talking to him.
- You can do a short comment and a follow-up comment.

Which comment is more closely related to the speaker's topic?

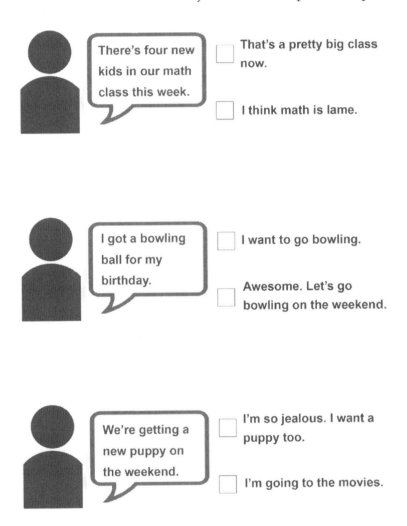

There's four new kids in our math class this week.

☐ That's a pretty big class now.

☐ I think math is lame.

I got a bowling ball for my birthday.

☐ I want to go bowling.

☐ Awesome. Let's go bowling on the weekend.

We're getting a new puppy on the weekend.

☐ I'm so jealous. I want a puppy too.

☐ I'm going to the movies.

Which comment is more closely related to the speaker's topic?

I got new shoes. What do you think?

☐ My shoes are too tight.

☐ They look great!

I've got cookies to share today.

☐ Yumm. Thanks a ton!

☐ I had cookies yesterday.

We might go to Hawaii for Christmas.

☐ Hawaii has several islands.

☐ Wow. That would be awesome.

Which comment is more closely related to the speaker's topic?

I'm going to be a vampire for Halloween.

☐ Cool. I'm going to be a skeleton.

☐ Halloween is next week.

Have you tasted coffee?

☐ Yeah. Coffee contains caffeine.

☐ Yeah. I didn't like it much.

Our dog was sick on the weekend.

☐ That doesn't sound good.

☐ Dogs often get sick if they eat bad food.

Which comment is more closely related to the speaker's topic?

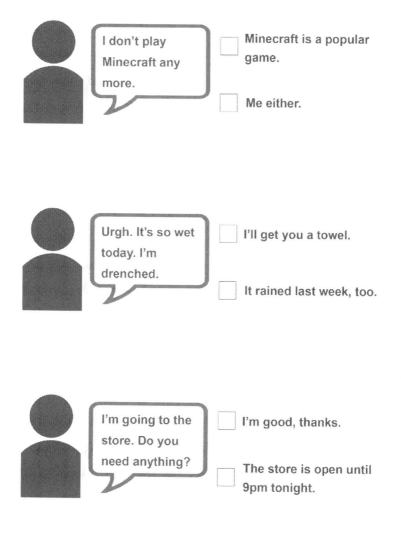

I don't play Minecraft any more.

☐ Minecraft is a popular game.

☐ Me either.

Urgh. It's so wet today. I'm drenched.

☐ I'll get you a towel.

☐ It rained last week, too.

I'm going to the store. Do you need anything?

☐ I'm good, thanks.

☐ The store is open until 9pm tonight.

Which comment is more closely related to the speaker's topic?

I'm so excited about tonight.

☐ Have a great time at the game!

☐ My dog has fleas.

Did you like my joke?

☐ My dad likes to tell jokes.

☐ It was funny!

My grandma is going to teach me to fish.

☐ I like eating fish.

☐ That's cool. I'd love to learn to fish.

Add a comment that is related to the speaker's topic.

Add a comment that is related to the speaker's topic.

My favorite
subject is
science.

Hey, there's Eva
with her mom.

I'm going on an
airplane for the
first time.

Add a comment that is related to the speaker's topic.

Add a comment that is related to the speaker's topic.

Add a comment that is related to the speaker's topic.

Add a comment.

Add a comment.

Add a comment.

Add a comment.

I like snow better than rain.

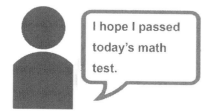

I hope I passed today's math test.

Let's get a big popcorn when we go to the movies.

Add a comment.

FOLLOW-UP COMMENTS: REVIEW

My comment was related.

My comment focused on my friend's topic, not my special interest.

I oriented my body or used eye contact.

ADD A FOLLOW-UP QUESTION

A follow-up question is a question that is related to the current topic of conversation.

Along with follow-up comments, follow-up questions are a key tool for maintaining a conversation. It is a vital skill for your learner.

In this section, your student learns how to ask appropriate, on-topic follow-up questions that are interesting to their conversation partner.

As illustrated in the following example, follow-up questions can be preceded by a short comment - but it is not necessary.

A: We went camping on the weekend.
B: Cool. Where did you go?

WHAT:

- A **follow-up question** is a question that asks for more details about what your friend just said.

WHY:

- Follow-up questions let you learn more about what your friend is interested in.
- Follow-up questions show you are listening. Speakers feel good when they know you are interested.

HOW:

- Your question must be **related** to what your friend just said.
- Your question should ask for **new** information - not something you already know.
- Your question should be related to **your friend's topic**, not your own special interest.
- Use **'open' questions** that start with WHEN, WHERE, WHY, WHAT, HOW, etc.
- Avoid too many 'Yes/No' questions in a row.
- Occasionally, **look at your friend briefly** when you begin the question so he knows you are talking to him.

- You can do a follow-up comment **and** a follow-up question. Conversation is pretty flexible.

Which question is related?

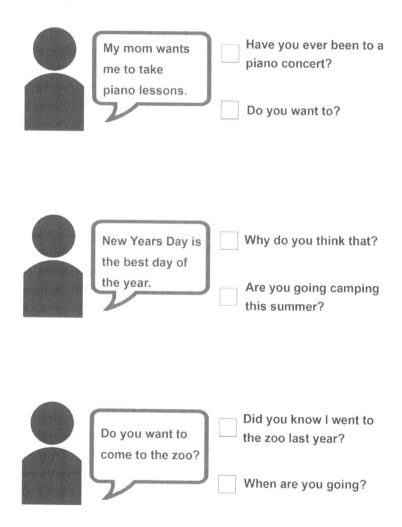

My mom wants me to take piano lessons.

☐ Have you ever been to a piano concert?

☐ Do you want to?

New Years Day is the best day of the year.

☐ Why do you think that?

☐ Are you going camping this summer?

Do you want to come to the zoo?

☐ Did you know I went to the zoo last year?

☐ When are you going?

Which question is related?

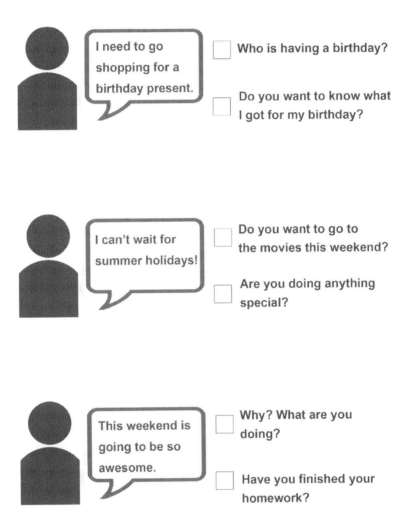

Which question is related?

I'm going to make hot dogs for dinner tonight.

☐ Regular hot dogs or chili dogs?

☐ Are you going on the field trip tomorrow?

My friend Sue is moving to Kansas.

☐ When is she leaving?

☐ I know the capital of Kansas. Do you want me to tell you?

My cat is going to have kittens soon.

☐ Have you see the Lion King movie?

☐ Are you going to keep them?

Which question is related?

My mom has signed me up for math tutoring.

☐ Are you watching the game on Sunday?

☐ I do tutoring. What center will you go to?

The pool opens this weekend.

☐ Yay! Are you going?

☐ Are you going to the mall this weekend?

My brother goes to college this weekend.

☐ When does college basketball start?

☐ He's going to Indiana State, right?

Which question is related?

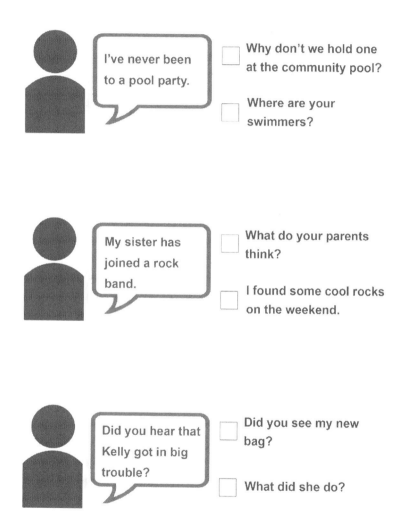

I've never been to a pool party.

☐ Why don't we hold one at the community pool?

☐ Where are your swimmers?

My sister has joined a rock band.

☐ What do your parents think?

☐ I found some cool rocks on the weekend.

Did you hear that Kelly got in big trouble?

☐ Did you see my new bag?

☐ What did she do?

Ask a question that is related.

Ask a question that is related.

Ask a question that is related.

Ask a question that is related.

Ask a question that is related.

Which question asks for new information?

☐ What has Ms B done now?

☐ Who are you talking about?

☐ What game did you play?

☐ What was the score?

Which question asks for new information?

☐ What movie did you see?

☐ What was your favorite part?

☐ Have you bought your plane tickets yet?

☐ What are your plans for summer?

Which question asks for new information?

Thanks! How did your collage work out?

Thanks! What did you do for the art assignment?

Do they often do that?

Are they arguing again?

Which question asks for new information?

☐ Yay! Did you smile at him?

☐ Who looked at you?

☐ Do you walk him to school?

☐ When will he be old enough to walk by himself?

Which question asks for new information?

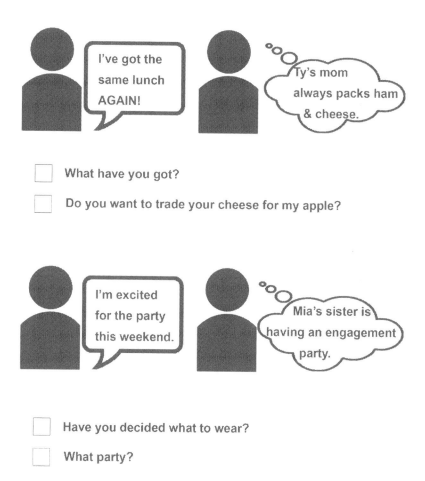

What have you got?

Do you want to trade your cheese for my apple?

Have you decided what to wear?

What party?

Ask a question that makes use of the information you already know.

Ask a question that makes use of the information you already know.

Ask a question that makes use of the information you already know.

Ask a question that makes use of the information you already know.

Ask a question that makes use of the information you already know.

Come up with 5 possible follow-up questions to continue the conversation. (Hint: Use Who, What, Where, Why, How, etc)

Science is confusing.

_____

_____

_____

_____

_____

My mom is going to buy a new car.

_____

_____

_____

_____

_____

Come up with 5 possible follow-up questions to continue the conversation. (Hint: Use Who, What, Where, Why, How, etc)

My dog has fleas.

_____

_____

_____

_____

_____

My mom wants me to do hip-hop dancing.

_____

_____

_____

_____

_____

Come up with 5 possible follow-up questions to continue the conversation. (Hint: Use Who, What, Where, Why, How, etc)

Fortnite is the best!

_____

_____

_____

_____

_____

Ugh. These shoes are too small. I need to get new ones.

_____

_____

_____

_____

_____

Come up with 5 possible follow-up questions to continue the conversation. (Hint: Use Who, What, Where, Why, How, etc)

I went hiking on the weekend.

_____

_____

_____

_____

_____

My mom and dad had a big fight yesterday.

_____

_____

_____

_____

_____

Come up with 5 possible follow-up questions to continue the conversation. (Hint: Use Who, What, Where, Why, How, etc)

I broke my mom's favorite vase last night.

_____

_____

_____

_____

_____

My dad is taking me to a soccer game tonight!

_____

_____

_____

_____

_____

Come up with 5 possible follow-up questions to continue the conversation. (Hint: Use Who, What, Where, Why, How, etc)

I wish I had more games for my Xbox.

_____

_____

_____

_____

_____

I'm worried my dad might lose his job.

_____

_____

_____

_____

_____

Come up with 5 possible follow-up questions to continue the conversation. (Hint: Use Who, What, Where, Why, How, etc)

Come up with 5 possible follow-up questions to continue the conversation. (Hint: Use Who, What, Where, Why, How, etc)

> There's a substitute teacher today.

_____

_____

_____

_____

_____

> My teacher brought her hamster to class.

_____

_____

_____

_____

_____

Come up with 5 possible follow-up questions to continue the conversation. (Hint: Use Who, What, Where, Why, How, etc)

> The Reptile Guy is coming to my birthday party.

_____

_____

_____

_____

> I made the soccer team!

_____

_____

_____

_____

Come up with 5 possible follow-up questions to continue the conversation. (Hint: Use Who, What, Where, Why, How, etc)

_____

_____

_____

_____

_____

_____

_____

_____

_____

Add a follow-up question.

My little sister just did something really funny.

I got a new ipad.

I have a ton of homework tonight.

Add a follow-up question.

Add a follow-up question.

My dad's cooking a roast tonight.

Seattle is my favorite city by far.

I don't want to go to camp this summer.

Add a follow-up question.

Add a follow-up question.

FOLLOW-UP QUESTIONS: REVIEW

My question was related.

My question asked for new information.

My questions were mostly open questions.

I oriented my body or used eye contact.

MULTI-TURN
CONVERSATIONS

A conversation consists of a series of turns where participants add follow-up comments and questions related to the current topic.

Now that your student can successfully add short comments, follow-up comments and follow-up questions, they are ready for multi-turn conversations.

This section provides incremental targets for you and your student to aim for. Each page provides a turn target and sample topics.

Have fun talking with your learner!

Choose a topic and start a conversation. Try to reach two turns each using any combination of short comments, follow-up comments and follow-up questions.

Favorite Video Game

Favorite Superhero

Favorite Candy

Favorite Teacher

Favorite Animal

Favorite Sport

Choose a topic and start a conversation. Try to reach two turns each using any combination of short comments, follow-up comments and follow-up questions.

If I could get a new pet, it would be a...

If I was a teacher, I would teach...

If I owned a restaurant, it would serve...

If I had one wish, I would wish for...

If I had a million dollars, I would...

If I could fly, I would...

If I could see one day in the future, the day I would choose...

Choose a topic and start a conversation. Try to reach three turns each using any combination of short comments, follow-up comments and follow-up questions.

I would like to meet...

Would you rather be a fruit or a vegetable?

If I had a time machine...

My favorite day of the year is...

If I had a superpower, it would be...

The grossest thing I have ever seen is...

If I could buy any car, I would buy a...

Choose a topic and start a conversation. Try to reach three turns each using any combination of short comments, follow-up comments and follow-up questions.

One sport I would like to try is...

My favorite place to visit is...

If I could design my dream house, it would include...

My favorite breakfast includes...

The first thing I do after I wake up is...

The best thing about my school is...

My favorite dessert is...

Choose a topic and start a conversation. Try to reach four turns each using any combination of short comments, follow-up comments and follow-up questions.

If I could design an awesome back yard, it would include...

The best day of my life was...

My favorite shoes are...

When I am on the computer, my favorite activity is...

My favorite joke is...

I once went to hospital and...

If I had to become an animal, I would choose to be...

Choose a topic and start a conversation. Try to reach four turns each using any combination of short comments, follow-up comments and follow-up questions.

My favorite shirt is...

One time at the dentist I...

I would love to meet...

A perfect picnic would include...

How much weekly allowance should kids get?

A country I would like to visit is...

My favorite book is...

Choose a topic and start a conversation. Try to reach five turns each using any combination of short comments, follow-up comments and follow-up questions.

I wish I could cook...

My favorite summer camp would include...

For my mom's birthday I would like to give her...

The chore I hate most is...

My favorite hobby is...

My favorite drink is...

If I could order any meal, I would choose...

Choose a topic and start a conversation. Try to reach five turns each using any combination of short comments, follow-up comments and follow-up questions.

I am really good at...

I am really terrible at...

After school I like to...

With my dad, I love to...

The season I like best is...

If I could invent an ice cream flavor, it would be...

My favorite pizza toppings are...

Choose a topic and start a conversation. Try to reach six turns each using any combination of short comments, follow-up comments and follow-up questions.

I like to listen to...

If I could get anything for my birthday, it would be...

If I was the star in a movie, it would be about...

When I grow up, I will...

If I had a pet robot, it would be able to...

My favorite vegetable is...

My favorite season is...

Choose a topic and start a conversation. Try to reach six turns each using any combination of short comments, follow-up comments and follow-up questions.

Would you rather live at the beach or in the mountains?

I would like to be famous for...

The most interesting thing about me is...

If I could choose to be someone else for a day, I would choose...

The best thing about my neighborhood is...

Another language I would like to speak is...

My favorite place to visit is...

BEFORE YOU GO

If you found this book useful, please leave a short review on Amazon. It makes an amazing difference for independent publishers like Happy Frog Press. Just two sentences will do!

Don't forget to look for other workbooks in the **Six-Minute Thinking Skills** series, publishing in 2018 & 2019.

Your learners might also benefit from our **Six-Minute Social Skills series**.

The workbooks in this series build core social skills for kids who have social skills challenges, such as those with Autism, Asperger's and ADHD.

Although numbered, these books can be used in any order.

CERTIFICATE
OF
ACHIEVEMENT

THIS CERTIFICATE IS AWARDED TO

_____

IN RECOGNITION OF

_____

_____	_____
DATE	SIGNATURE

Made in the USA
Coppell, TX
19 April 2022

76786099R00055